COOL CAREERS WITHOUT COLLEGE

CAREERS FOR PEOPLE WHO LOVE CRAFTING

Siyavush Saidian

ROSEN PUBLISHING

New York

Published in 2021 by The Rosen Publishing Group, Inc.
29 East 21st Street, New York, NY 10010

First Edition

Portions of this work were originally authored by Stephanie Mannino and published as *Cool Careers Without College for People Who Love Crafts*. All new material in this edition authored by Siyavush Saidian.

Library of Congress Cataloging-in-Publication Data

Names: Saidian, Siyavush, author.
Title: Careers for people who love crafting / Siyavush Saidian.
Description: New York : Rosen Publishing, [2021] |
Series: Cool careers without college | Includes bibliographical references and index.
Identifiers: LCCN 2020008606 | ISBN 9781499468779 (library binding) | ISBN 9781499468762 (paperback)
Subjects: LCSH: Handicraft—Vocational guidance—Juvenile literature.
Classification: LCC TT149 .S23 2020 | DDC 745.5023—dc23
LC record available at https://lccn.loc.gov/2020008606

Some of the images in this book illustrate individuals who are models. The depictions do not imply actual situations or events.

Manufactured in the United States of America

CONTENTS

INTRODUCTION

In the modern world, it seems like everything—from everyday basics to high-end luxuries—are made by machines. Most people who make things with their hands do so only as a hobby. Most weavers, quilters, framers, and other crafters never make money from their products. Instead, they work because they're passionate about what they do. But what if you wanted to make a career out of crafting? It can be tough, but it's undoubtedly possible—and you can have success even without an advanced education.

This may sound too good to be true, and there are definitely some things you need to do before you can break into the crafting industry. First, it's absolutely essential that you have a passion for whatever art form you specialize in. Whether you could spend all day weaving baskets, nailing frames, or shaping wood, it's important that you're dedicated to your work. Second, you'll need to learn from others. That means you'll spend a lot of time reading at the library, researching online, or attending classes at a local community college or recreation center. Third, you'll have to decide how you'll actually turn your new skills into a full-time career. Many crafters, from floral artists to stained glass makers, are self-employed, setting their own work schedules and selling products online or at arts festivals. Others work for an existing business, making a bit less money but having better financial security.

Still others craft only part-time, supplementing their income by teaching their art to others. The world of crafting can be rewarding—both personally and financially—if you play your cards right.

If you're unsure about what field of crafting you may want to explore—or you're curious about what your next step should be—your best resource will be other professionals. Most crafters are proud artists, and they'll be more than happy to give advice to someone from the next generation who will carry on their handiwork traditions. In addition to professional trade organizations, which represent and educate crafters of all kinds, many cities and towns feature industry conventions and informal local meetings of likeminded artists. No matter your area of interest, from calligraphy to quilting, there are others like you who can help you get started down the rewarding path of crafting.

CHAPTER 1

BE A BASKET CASE

Did you know that basket weaving is one of the world's oldest crafts? Talented ancient artists borrowed techniques used to make shelters to create a new item: the humble basket. These containers, made from natural materials such as grasses and bamboo, have had countless uses over the years. They've been part of religious ceremonies and used to carry food for picnics. A well-made basket is a versatile and durable piece of functional art. If you're interested in carrying on ancient traditions, a career as a basket weaver may be right for you.

A DELICATE CRAFT

If you want to become a basket weaver, you'll need to have a great sense of touch. Good hand-eye coordination is also essential. Creating a basket, either from scratch or by following a pattern, can take hours, days, or weeks, so it's important that the basket maker be patient and able to stick to the task at hand.

Baskets can be made out of all kinds of materials. Once chosen, the base material is woven or coiled to form the basket. Reeds, splint, and wild vines—which tend to be long and sturdy—are the materials of choice if you want to weave. Shorter materials, such as pine needles and grass, are most commonly coiled because they're more delicate. These are the kinds of considerations you'll have to keep in mind as a basket maker.

If you're interested in making baskets for a living, starting with the Shaker style is always a good choice.

There are dozens of basket types you can create using weaving or coiling techniques. Shaker baskets, which are made in simple, elegant styles, have maintained their popularity over the course of decades. Named for a religious group in the United States that made these baskets until 1925, many amateur and professional basket weavers construct their products in this enduring style.

PREPARE TO CRAFT

Some handicrafts require a lot of time investment, financial investment, and highly advanced skills—even for beginners. Basket making is fortunately not one of those crafts. Many professional basket weavers watched their parents or grandparents practicing the craft, learning bits and pieces of the process as they grew up. Others may have started crafting simply as a hobby and found a talent for basket weaving. No matter how you personally get interested in the art of basketry, there are many affordable options for you to learn and improve.

If you're an absolute beginner, try heading down to your local hobby store to look for a kit that contains instructions and materials for your first project. Though this may seem old-fashioned, do-it-yourself kits like this have helped train generations of aspiring crafters. They often contain everything you need—in one box—to embark on your basketwork journey. If you have access to your own materials, you can try finding prints and directions online.

Once you have most of the basics down, you should try to look for opportunities or education. One of the best ways to learn about basket making—and most other crafts—is to learn from an experienced maker who can pass along their years of wisdom and experience. Check out nearby community colleges, recreation centers, and adult education programs to see if there are any upcoming or ongoing basketry courses. If that's not an option, try talking to parents or grandparents—your own or your friends'—to see if they know anything about how to work with baskets. You may be surprised how much you can learn.

A CRAFTY LIVING

Though there are some companies that employ full-time basket makers, most people who work in this field are self-employed. This can mean many things, and you'll have a lot of options if you want to enter the world of basketry. If you're willing to travel, you can craft baskets and sell them at arts festivals around your state. If you're really successful, you can even sell across the country. A similar option is to sell your work online, either through a personal website or a digital marketplace. Be aware, however, that if you sell baskets over the internet, you'll be responsible for arranging shipping and handling, as well as paying any taxes and fees that go along with e-commerce.

Instead of bringing their products to the world, some craftspeople wait for customers to come to

The baskets you make can be as simple or as complex as you'd like. If you want to make money, you'll have to balance the time it takes to make each basket against how much you can sell it for.

them. This means they make a few sample products, post pictures and testimonials online, and encourage potential clients to contact them. They then work with the client to design a basket, negotiate a price, and deliver the final product. Working like this can often net you more money per basket sold since you're custom-making a craft for someone, but your pay may not be as consistent.

If you become highly skilled and you're a good communicator, you may want to consider teaching others. Just as you may have learned from a master by taking a local class, you can pass your talents and advice on to others. Positions like this can be hard to come by, but teaching your craft is a great way to encourage others to try it out.

According to the Bureau of Labor Statistics, the job outlook for craftspeople is a little rough, with a projected 1 percent growth between 2018 and 2028 (compared to the national average of 5 percent). However, if you can prove your skills online or in person, there's little doubt you'll be able to weave together a client base to support your career.

CHAPTER 2

BOOKS THAT BIND

When considering what makes up a book, most people probably think of the pages that hold the title's content. However, the covers and spine of a book can be just as artfully crafted as the words on its pages. Bookbinders are highly specialized craftspeople whose job it is to find ways to artistically—and creatively—tie all the pages of a manuscript together.

BIND 'EM UP

The basic job of a bookbinder—particularly one who does hand binding—is to either decoratively bind paper for a custom book or repair an existing title. Though one of these specializations may seem more interesting to you than the other, chances are high that you'll have to be able to do both if you want to succeed. Because most books are mass-produced, being printed and bound at the same time by large machines in print shops all over the world, there's a decreasing need for hand binders. However, people and businesses making one-off special editions of certain books often turn to a craftsperson to make their unique product stand out. In between custom work like this, however, you'll likely have to focus on book repair and binding replacement.

Over time, books are subject to wear and tear caused by many factors, including repeated opening and closing, rough handling, unfriendly climate, and simple old age. Treasured family heirlooms, such as old yearbooks or irreplaceable editions of important works of literature—including first editions of rare books—often need to be repaired at some point. This is especially true of very old editions of classic volumes.

If any of that sounds like something you'd like to do, you may have the makings of a bookbinder. Many professionals in this industry have been entranced by books since childhood. Maybe you have a favorite story you've always liked to read, or maybe your family had a large collection of older books with their distinctive paper aroma. Maybe you're just good with your hands and you'd like to get paid to flex your skills. No matter the reason, bookbinding can be a highly satisfying career.

There are many ways to bind books, and your skill as a bookbinder will be measured not only by how many you know, but how well you execute them. For example, you may know that saddle stitching involves stapling the pages of a book, but do all of your saddle-stitched products have equal spacing between staples? Many people have heard of spiral

Bookbinding is an old-school craft, with even its modern masters using old-fashioned tools. Historical techniques combined with present-day skills can make books bound by hand truly special for your clients.

binding, but do your spiral-bound books have clean, straight wires? Getting the details right is a big part of achieving success in this field.

PREPARE TO CRAFT

Believe it or not, if you want to break into the field of bookbinding, there are educational training programs specifically for that purpose. There are even bookbinding schools that can start teaching you the skills you'll need to have success in the business. It takes a lot of time, energy, and practice to become a true pro, and attending a bookbinding course can help accelerate your learning process.

However, you don't necessarily have to go to a trade school to become a crafter. There are professional associations all across the United States that can help connect you with existing professionals. You may also want to look into online and print publications that can teach you the basics of bookbinding. Some basic artistic and scientific knowledge can also help set you on the right path. You should have a basic understanding of art history, literature, chemistry, and geometry. These skills will all help you when you actually start working with books.

THE *F* WORDS

There are a lot of important industry terms you should know if you want to become a bookbinder, but two are especially important: forwarding and finishing. In this field, forwarding refers to the process of assembling a book. It includes folding the sheets of paper into pages and sewing them together. It also involves constructing the cover and attaching the pages and endpapers to it. Finishing, on the other hand, refers to embellishing the cover with the book's title and some extra decorations. Finishing can include tooling the cover or adding inlays or any other artistic touch the bookbinder chooses.

Skilled bookbinders are able to put their own personal touch on their projects, coming up with elaborate and beautiful designs.

Though the learning curve for becoming a bookbinder can feel intimidating, it's a crafting technique that anyone with good hand-eye coordination can master. Once you start practicing, you'll quickly improve. You shouldn't be afraid to apply creative or experimental solutions to your projects because that's part of what makes bookbinding such a satisfying career. Because you'll likely be working with old books regularly, you should also have an interest in old literature and a respect for history. You must have a professional and helpful attitude as you're working with clients whose books need your artistic touch.

A CRAFTY LIVING

When you think you're ready to make money as a bookbinder, there are several paths you can follow. The more traditional practice is to find work for another business, often called a bindery. In this position, you'd likely be assigned to benchwork, which includes the physical tasks involved with bookbinding. You'd spend most of your time removing old bindings, repairing books, assembling new books, and creating and placing covers. Because this is entry-level work, you shouldn't expect to make a lot of money. However, working for an established business gives you a level of security that's missing from another popular option: self-employment.

A self-employed bookbinder is just that: someone who accepts binding work from clients and keeps the revenue after expenses and taxes are paid. If you try this out, you'll be setting your own prices and schedule. This often means you'll be able to make more money for the same amount of work done if you worked for someone else. However, you may not have a steady stream of clients, you'd have to buy all the equipment yourself, and you'd have to deal with customers who don't pay—without anyone to back you up. These are all important aspects of the job you'll have to consider before making the decision to work for yourself.

The outlook for jobs in the bookbinding industry is uncertain. Though handcrafted work is still appreciated by many consumers, internet shopping and mass production of books have damaged the binding business. After all, it's much cheaper to buy a paperback online or flip through an e-book on your phone than go out and find a decorated hardcover copy of a classic novel. However, there will always be a place in the world for a talented craftsperson. So long as you're willing to learn the skills, you should be able to find work at a bindery, library, university, or as a self-employed bookbinder.

CHAPTER 3

MORE THAN WRITING

At the most basic level, calligraphy is fancy writing. For people who appreciate the intricate lettering—and the artists themselves—this craft is so much more. Calligraphy has a long history, and some prominent examples of the art have come from the Middle East, Japan, India, and China. Ancient calligraphers used brushes and ink to make their designs, and these tools are sometimes still used in modern times. However, with the rise of technology, including advanced art software, there's never been a better time to be a digital calligraphy designer.

WITH A FLOURISH

The work of a calligrapher is highly distinctive, and you've probably seen and appreciated their art without even knowing it. A calligrapher creates attractive lettering on documents, signs, or anything else that's especially significant. Think of the last time you saw the envelope for a wedding invitation or a diploma

written with beautiful, flowing letters. Because each letter is created by hand, calligraphy is a slow, painstaking process. It's not a good career choice for an impatient person. However, if you have an artistic talent, the patience to slowly study, and the desire to practice this art form, calligraphy can be extremely rewarding.

Calligraphy can help to create a special mood of joy, elegance, and importance. The hand lettering of calligraphy can make the smallest details—such as place cards at a wedding—even more special.

People hire calligraphers because they want their documents, signs, or other printed pieces to stand out and have a distinctive, distinguished appearance. A calligrapher may work on their own—in a self-owned business—or perhaps provide services through a larger graphics company. Working for yourself has its advantages and disadvantages when compared to traditional employment. Also keep in mind that if you work for another company, you may need to acquire skills in addition to calligraphy.

Though it has ancient origins, calligraphy can still be seen all around the contemporary world.

PREPARE TO CRAFT

Practice, practice, and more practice will be the key to learning about calligraphy. Using nothing but basic pens and pencils, you can practice your penmanship. Handwriting is the foundation of calligraphy. If your regular handwriting is sloppy, your calligraphy work will be sloppy too. Practice making your lines straight, your curves symmetrical, and your letters even. Once you have the standard characters down, you can try to make more detailed versions of each symbol. One of the most important parts of a calligrapher's job is being consistent—each letter should look the same every time it appears.

Once you have some basic hands-on practice behind you, it may be worthwhile to look into calligraphy classes. Check out a local community college or recreation center to see if there are any related courses available. Even if you can't find anything that specifically teaches calligraphy, a basic art class can teach you some valuable principles, such as color theory and basic aesthetic design. Combined with your handwriting practice, this training should serve you well as you try to become a professional calligrapher.

A CRAFTY LIVING

If you want to find work as a calligrapher, you'll have to be open-minded about your compensation. Especially if you work as an independent freelancer—as many calligraphers do—you'll have to accept that certain projects simply don't pay as much as others. For example, you may set up an online store selling your calligraphic services. You'll probably get a lot of orders for inexpensive products, such as a bookmark with someone's name written in calligraphy. Though you should also list big-ticket items—such as a fully

THE FALL AND RISE OF CALLIGRAPHY

Before the age of computers and keyboards, anyone who wanted anything written down had to write it by hand. Paper and ink have also been precious resources throughout much of history. This meant people took a lot of time and care about writing things down. If you look at old books and documents, you'll immediately be able to see the intricate lettering that went into everyday life. With the invention of the typewriter in 1867, however, beautiful penmanship became less important. In the 20th century, calligraphy supporters created a renewed interest in the art. While visiting the United States in 1974, well-known English calligrapher Donald Jackson taught lectures and workshops on the art. He also did television interviews during his visit, encouraging Americans to form their own calligraphy societies. His enthusiasm for the craft caught on. Today, there are dozens of calligraphic societies in the United States and Europe.

custom sign or a set of wedding invitations and place cards—you can't expect these to sell as well or as frequently, even though they're worth more money.

If you don't want to strike out on your own, print shops, craft stores, schools, colleges, and publishers hire calligraphers. Greeting card companies also sometimes hire in-house calligraphers to design the latest card styles. However, finding full-time work in this industry can be difficult, so you should be willing to try self-employment if you can't find a job right away.

Invitations and place settings for important events, including weddings and fundraisers, often use a calligrapher's work to set a tone of refinement and elegance.

You should also keep in mind that calligraphy, like most artistic fields, is highly competitive. Because you don't need an advanced education to sell your skills, it's an appealing occupation for many young people. If you want to stand out from the crowd, whether you're applying for an in-house position at a company or just trying to make money by selling online, your calligraphy has to be clean, refined, and consistent. If you're self-employed, it's important to know your limits. If a client is asking for work you don't think you can handle, don't be afraid to turn the work down. It's better to miss out on a big job than do bad work and harm your reputation. On the flip side, if you consistently do great work for people, they'll likely leave positive reviews for you online, which can help drive business to your digital storefront.

CHAPTER 4

CLAY TIME

Pottery and ceramics are both art forms with rich histories that are deeply connected to human civilization. From ancient societies in which pottery was part of everyday life to modern times when decorative ceramics abound, the people whose hands can work clay into beautiful and useful constructions have been in high demand. If you liked to play with modeling compounds as a kid or you enjoy visualizing and crafting three-dimensional structures, becoming a potter or ceramist may be the perfect job for you.

NATURAL MATERIALS

Clay is an ancient natural material that's often found along banks of streams and rivers. Natural clay is available in a wide variety of colors, including white, brown, yellow, gray, red, blue, and black. Professional ceramists and potters don't use clay right out of the ground, of course. They buy clay that's been cleaned of pebbles and grit. The clay potters use is mixed with other ingredients to make it suitable for artistic use.

There are many similarities between pottery and ceramics, the most important of which is the use of clay. This material is common to both crafts. However, ceramics refers generally to any item that's made from a natural material and then fired at a high temperature to increase strength and durability. Ceramic products can be made out of other materials, while pottery is limited to just clay. In short, all pottery is ceramic, but not all ceramics are pottery.

Pottery is sometimes called earthenware, which simply means an object made out of clay. Earthenware is soft and porous when fired, unlike most ceramic products, which are typically much stronger after being heated. Nearly all ceramic or earthenware creations must be coated with glaze and fired again (often several times) to decorate and seal the surfaces. Glazes can be transparent or opaque, clear, or colored. They can be used to create a variety of surface finishes, from matte to shiny.

Before beginning a project, a ceramist must knead their clay to eliminate air bubbles trapped inside. They check their material for air bubbles by cutting through it. If the clay contains imperfections, no matter how small, it can fall apart or explode under the stress of firing. Spending extra time at the start of a project can prevent wasting time later on, and it makes workshops much safer.

Ceramics are easily recognizable by their shiny finishes, which are determined by the type of glaze used to seal the clay.

Some people build their designs by hand, while others fashion them on a potter's wheel. Using a potter's wheel may look easy—and its products can be beautiful—but it takes a lot of practice to master it. When you're just starting out, you should work on your ability to craft something by hand. Then, when you're more advanced, you can take those basic skills

and apply them to the potter's wheel.

Ceramists and potters most often work in studios, which are located in their homes or in a shared space with other artists. Either way, a studio should be an area fitted with worktables, a kiln, and many other kinds of equipment. Some spaces may allow you to rent or lease the bigger equipment, such as the kiln. This can help reduce your overall costs.

You can probably imagine a lot of items that are made by ceramists and potters. Coffee mugs, plates, jars, pots, bowls, and vases are all earthenware or ceramic products. People who earn their living from their pottery commonly design and craft their own distinct lines of products. If you want to become a potter, you'll have to be willing to practice and improve your designs.

Some ceramists and potters produce their designs in volume. This typically means their designs are more basic and focus on functionality, making them easier to craft. Other crafters specialize in one-of-a-kind pieces. Unique designs often take far more time to make and cost far more money. Ceramists and potters sell their work from their workshops, at craft shows and fairs, or online. If you become highly popular in your area, boutique art shops may even want to carry your products.

PREPARE TO CRAFT

If you're interested in trying to make a living by working with ceramics or pottery, you have several options. First and foremost, check in with a local community college to see if it's offering classes. Some traditional colleges and universities offer evening classes for the general public through continuing education programs. Fortunately, you don't need to be a full-time student to participate in these continuing education classes. You'll likely have to pay a one-time fee to complete a training program, but you'll have the benefit of learning from the college's faculty, using professional-grade equipment, and getting to connect with others who are interested in the craft.

Pottery is a popular craft, which means you'll likely be able to find classes that can teach you the basics alongside other beginners.

If you can't find any courses at a college, community arts organizations sometimes offer classes in ceramics and pottery, as do professional ceramics

KNOW YOUR MATERIALS

If you're going to become a professional artist, it's important that you know exactly what you're working with. Here are some basic definitions:

- Earthenware clay is opaque and slightly porous. It can be found in a wide range of colors, including white. When people talk about pottery, they're often referring to earthenware.
- Stoneware is nonporous and stronger than earthenware. Because stoneware must be fired at extremely high temperatures, its colors are more subdued.
- Porcelain clay, which is white, is stronger than earthenware. When fired, thin porcelain is delicate and translucent. It has the smoothest texture of the three types of clay. Expensive china is made from porcelain.

studios. These organizations may also run intensive ceramics or pottery programs during the summer.

In addition to taking classes to learn more about the art of pottery and ceramics, you should read books and do online research before you try making it as a craftsperson. When you're ready to get hands-on experience and start practicing with real clay, you can use this knowledge to get a head start on other beginners.

A CRAFTY LIVING

Selling your wares at craft markets, arts festivals, and online are just some of the ways to earn money with ceramics. You may have seen businesses where customers can paint and decorate presculpted pottery, which is then fired by the professionals in the studio. Opening or working at a business like this is one way to advance your career in ceramics. Another way to earn money with ceramics is to teach others. You're not alone in your interest in ceramics, and once you've mastered the craft, there will certainly be others willing to learn from an experienced ceramist. Community centers and arts organizations offer classes for both kids and adults, so you can pass your skills on to another generation of artists.

CHAPTER 5

PAINTING AND DECORATING

Though the portraits and landscapes that hang in museums get a lot of attention, there are many uses of paint other than traditional artwork. Decorative painting has been around for thousands of years, dating back to some of the earliest human societies. If you have an eye for art, exploring a career in decorative or craft painting may be a good choice. Artists working in this field specialize in applying paint to many different kinds of materials, from windows to walls to signs and more. The work requires an attention to detail, a willingness to improvise, and talent with a brush.

A FRESH COAT OF PAINT

There are many different varieties of craft painting, each with their own learning curve. One type of decorative painting, for example, involves adding paint to existing household objects, such as walls, cabinets, and chairs. Adding a decorative design is one way to create unique, special pieces.

Another area of this craft is sign painting. Many sign painters still design and paint letters and graphic designs by hand on many kinds of signs. You've probably seen the work of an artist like this on a window sign or a billboard. If you've ever noticed the name of a business or person painted on a glass door, that's the work of a sign painter who used a brush and paint. Talented sign painters can run their own independent businesses, accepting jobs from various clients one at a time. There are also opportunities for sign painting as an employee at an existing company, such as one that prepares marketing materials or outdoor advertising for other businesses.

Stenciling, a technique used to decorate a surface with paint, has recently experienced a surge in popularity. Far from a new craft, stenciling dates as far back as the artwork of the ancient Egyptians. Other cultures also incorporated stenciling as an art form, although its exact origin is unknown.

A craft that's been popular in the United States since colonial times, stencils are today used to decorate furniture, walls, boxes, paper, fabric, and countless other surfaces. Visiting a specialized stencil shop—or the stencil department of an arts and craft supply store—will give you an idea of the huge variety of stencil patterns available. You may even get to take a practice lesson, as many stencil stores provide classes.

A QUICK PRACTICE RUN

If you think you might be interested in a job in the decorative painting industry, you should start by practicing with simple objects at home. Try using acrylic enamel paint to decorate small glass objects, such as drinking glasses, plates, or vases, with designs, sayings, or images. Get creative with it. Maybe make a birthday present for a friend by painting their name onto a drinking glass, or just try to fit as many flowers as you can onto a single plate. This field is all about artistic creativity and flexibility, so try out a bunch of different designs. After painting, you can make your designs permanent by baking the object for half an hour in an oven at 350°Fahrenheit (177°Celsius).

You can start practicing your craft painting skills by experimenting with small objects at home.

Once a stencil design has been cut out of stencil paper, the artist uses a stencil brush, a sponge, or a roller—sometimes all at once—to apply the design to the surface that's getting the fresh coat of paint. A stencil artist can move much more quickly than a painter who works freehand because the stenciler uses the same premade design over and over again. Many stencil artists use fast-drying acrylic paints that simplify the painting process and reduce wait times.

PREPARE TO CRAFT

If you want to get into decorative painting, be aware that the field is wide, deep, and highly varied. Your ability to make money will be affected not just by your pure artistic talent, but also by the number of styles and finishes you can execute. There are many traditional faux finishes you should learn to paint. There's also a variety of decorative styles, including French country, trompe l'oeil ("fool the eye"), and early American. It's a good idea to start off by taking classes in the areas or styles that interest you. You can also learn more about specific styles and techniques online or by reading art instructional books. No matter where and how you learn, you should also practice as much as you can, experimenting with styles and pushing your artistic limits.

In addition to your creativity, you also need to have good people skills if you work in decorative painting. Whether you're working for an established company or starting your own business, you'll likely

DOING IT BIG

A mural is a type of painting that's created on a grand scale. Often seen on the exteriors of buildings or interior walls, murals are much larger than traditional paintings that hang in homes and art galleries. Businesses often hire muralists to add a dynamic color statement to the outside of their buildings. Indoors, murals can help set a mood or be a conversation starter for clients or guests.

Before beginning to paint, a mural artist designs an image that's both appropriate to the project and the right size for the wall. Once the wall has been cleaned, sealed, and primed, the muralist transfers their design onto the wall. While traditional painters often sketch their vision onto a canvas, muralists are dealing with much larger spaces. Instead of sketching, muralists can work from a grid design, with a projector that throws an image of the drawing onto the wall. Some artists prefer to freehand paint, working around any mistakes or missteps.

Fresco painting is a type of mural that's painted on a wet plaster wall. To create a fresco, a painter makes a full-scale drawing of their vision, fastens it to the wall, and presses the outlines into the plaster. These outlines will be used as a guide when applying the paint. Fresco painting is often done with watercolors, as they run into the wet plaster more effectively than other paint types.

Muralists are highly skilled decorative painters that work on a large scale.

have to interact with clients who have specific wants and needs with their commissions.

A CRAFTY LIVING

Because it can be tough to get your start in this field—and art is a difficult industry to begin with—you shouldn't expect to make huge paychecks early on in your career. It's more important to set long-term goals, both professionally and financially. Of course, the more you learn about the industry and the better your skills become, the more money you can command, whether you're self-employed or working for someone else.

If you're struggling to make it as a full-time decorative painter, teaching is a wonderful way to help others learn the craft while keeping your own skills fresh. In addition, decorative painters often branch out into other fields. Many have become art product salespeople, designers, authors of instructional books, and demonstrators at craft shows or fairs. Keep your options open and you'll be able to make a living doing what you love.

CHAPTER 6

FLOWERING BUSINESS

Few things have captured human imagination throughout history more than flowers. In modern times, it's easy to head down to a supermarket and grab a beautiful bouquet of flowers. But have you ever thought about how someone chooses which flowers to place next to each other? The artists who organize and arrange flowers are called floral designers. In addition to bouquets, professionals in this field put together festive wreaths, eye-catching centerpieces, aromatic potpourri arrangements, and bold fashion accessories. Though traditional floral artisans work mainly with real live flowers, there's also room in this craft for silk or other artificial flowers and dried petals, depending on the type of arrangement you're interested in.

Arranging flowers may seem easy, but floral artists are skilled crafters who have to take every detail into account.

INEDIBLE ARRANGEMENTS

Flowers have long been considered the ultimate gift for showing appreciation and love. Just think of how many flowers are delivered each year to celebrate holidays, birthdays, and anniversaries. Because flowers hold sentimental value for so many people, there are a lot of opportunities to be found in the floral industry.

In addition to the flowers themselves, there are three basic elements that go into constructing a floral arrangement: the container, the plant material, and the mechanical components. Understanding these three items is one of the first steps to learning basic floral design.

Choosing the right container to hold an arrangement is rarely easy. Floral designers must keep in mind what their final product will look like and choose the container that will best complement the color, texture, and proportion of the arrangement. Depending on the desired effect, a container can be an integral part of the arrangement or just a vessel for the stars of the show: the actual flowers.

When designing a new floral arrangement, the craftsperson must first decide whether they'll use fresh flowers and plants, silk or artificial flowers, or dried petals and stems. There are a number of reasons to choose each of these materials, and the final choice will often come down to a client's preference. Most floral designers purchase their materials from wholesale suppliers.

The mechanical components of a floral arrangement include the base or armature that's placed inside the vase or container to hold the flower stems in place. For an understated look, neat and clean floral foam and chicken wire are often used. One popular way to hold plants in place is with a needle holder or pin holder (sometimes called a *kenzan*). Good needle holders are straight sided with a heavy lead base and an abundance of sharp, pointed, and closely spaced needles. When used properly, a needle holder will be nearly invisible, giving the flowers an appearance of naturally standing upright.

Designers often construct the foundation of the design by lining and filling a container. They use fresh plant material, decorative wood, or even wire, plastic, or rope. Filler plants, which have small blooms, can serve as a background for the main flowers in the arrangement. Baby's breath is often used for this purpose.

PREPARE TO CRAFT

If you're interested in exploring the floral industry, you can start out by working as an entry-level employee in a flower shop. Though you likely won't be handling advanced floral arrangements in this position, you can get hands-on experience handling flowers and

If you can find work at a flower shop, you'll be able to learn the ins and outs of plant care.

learning about the countless species available. If learning on the job is too intimidating, you can also get a good start by taking classes in floral arrangement. Look up local trade schools, community colleges, and botanical gardens to see if they're offering classes in floriculture or horticulture. You can also find many online tutorials on the basics of floral design, and you can practice some of these techniques in your own home.

Knowing a lot about design basics is a big part of professional flower arranging, but if you plan to open your own business, you'll encounter a different set of challenges. Learning about small business management and marketing can help you get your company off to a good start.

A CRAFTY LIVING

Salaries vary within the floral industry and largely depend on whether a designer works full- or part-time, alone, or for a large company. In general, you shouldn't expect to strike it rich in this business. What the industry lacks in compensation is made up for in passion.

Though handmade floral arrangements can be found at most weddings, fundraisers, and other big events, the outlook for this industry isn't great. The Bureau of Labor Statistics predicts that it will shrink by 14 percent between 2018 and 2028. This decline is mainly due to the spread of online flower delivery services and an increase in the number of grocery stores selling bouquets. However, though you may find it difficult to open your own floral arrangement business or work for an established florist, there are some options open to you. You can open an online shop, receiving custom orders and shipping your crafts all across the world. This will be easier if you focus on learning about arranging dried or artificial flowers, as shipping live plants can be difficult. A final concern to keep in mind: your workload as a floral designer will be seasonal. For example, people spend a lot of money on flowers during the winter holidays—especially Valentine's Day—and the wedding season in late summer, while the rest of the year sees much less demand.

CHAPTER 7

KEEP IT GLASSY

Glassmaking is both an art form and a technical challenge. From glassmakers, who use machines and tools to create their products, to glassblowers, who actually put their lips on the line, this industry is full of passionate craftspeople. If you want to be a part of this industry, you'll have to combine background knowledge, artistic talent, and creativity to make unique items with a personal flair. Do you have what it takes?

A FRAGILE ART

Glass has been an important part of human culture and society for thousands of years. Some of the oldest examples of glass, including decorative beads, detailed amulets, and highly adorned vases, have been found in the tombs of Egyptian pharaohs.

The earliest makers of glass created the product by melting a combination of silica and alkali. As the craft has advanced across countless

LOOKING AT GLASS HISTORY

Glass crafting has been around since prehistoric times. The first glass objects used by humans were made from natural glasses, such as obsidian (a black volcanic glass) or rock crystal. Ever since then, the craft of making and using glass has continually developed. The first glass factory in the United States was built in 1608, and the industry has flourished in the centuries since then. German-born manufacturer H. W. Stiegel produced some of the finest colonial glassware in his Pennsylvania factories. An American named Deming Jarves invented a glass-pressing machine around 1827. It was used in his Boston and Sandwich Glass Company. Jarves's innovative machine marked the beginning of mass-produced glass products. Traditional glassmakers were still able to earn a living making glass the old-fashioned way, despite the country embracing mass-produced glass. Fine craftsmanship was still highly valued.

generations, other substances have been used to improve the quality of glass. Today, glass is made by heating a chemical called flux—mixed with sand and an alkali—in a crucible at extremely hot temperatures. After the mixture has melted, the crucible is turned down, letting the glass cool to a lower—but still very hot—temperature.

If the glassmaker wants to create an object by blowing glass, they shape a glob of molten hot glass on the end of a punty, which is a special metal rod that's used to blow glass. The glassmaker blows into the punty, creating a bubble from the molten glass that's stuck to the end of the rod. When the

glassmaker is satisfied with the size of the bubble, they shape the hot glass with tools while twirling the glob to counteract the pull of gravity.

In the modern world, glass is used in architecture to transmit electricity; as an instrument in scientific research; and for lighting, optical instruments, and household utensils. Over the years, new forms of glass have revolutionized the profession of glassmaking. Safety glass, which is often constructed of two pieces of plate glass bonded together with a plastic that prevents the structure from shattering when broken, is one important innovation in glass technology.

Though glass has many practical uses, there's still a place for the craftsperson who uses glass to create objects of beauty and artistry. The unique pieces created by glassblowers offer something much more special than mass-produced objects.

PREPARE TO CRAFT

If you want to learn more about the art of glassmaking, you may have difficulty finding classes. Because the craft requires so much special equipment and training, it's not easy to find businesses or schools that allow amateurs in. However, you should still

Glassblowing is an ancient form of crafting, and it's necessary for making custom products.

try to find an introductory course at a local school, especially if it has on-site glassmaking facilities. If you know of a local glassmaker or a custom glass company, ask to become an apprentice. You might also ask glassmakers how they got started in the field and see if they can recommend any classes, online tutorials, or books to help you get started in the industry.

If you want to pursue this career, you'll need a lot of patience, dexterity, and precision. If you're a perfectionist who needs to get every detail of a project just right, glassmaking may be an appropriate field for you. On top of the artistic and creative skills you need to succeed as a glassmaker, you'll need to be able to tolerate exposure to intense heat, which is a natural part of the crafting process.

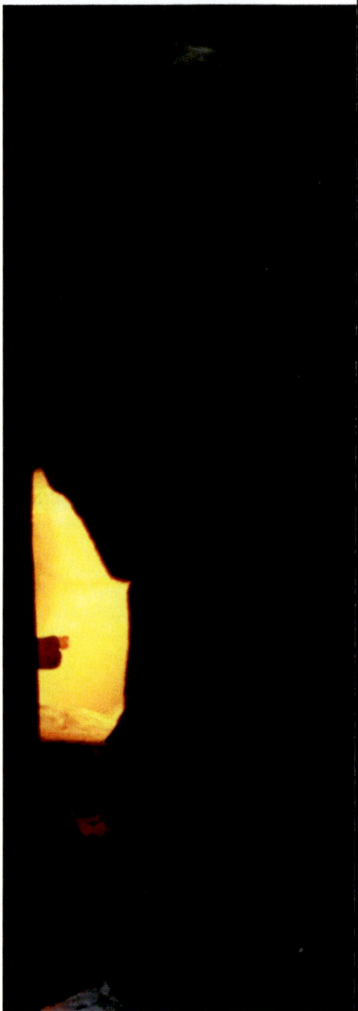

A CRAFTY LIVING

The amount of compensation you can expect to earn as a glass artisan is highly variable. If you can find a job as a full-time glassblower at an established company, you can make a fair amount of money. If you work as a self-employed artisan, your monthly income will be inconsistent, and you'll have to invest in some expensive equipment to make your products.

Glassblowing is a difficult and specialized craft. It takes a tremendous amount of determination, patience, and practice to learn. If you can master the craft of glassblowing, however, you can find

Before you start on your glassmaking journey, make sure you can stand the heat!

yourself in a deeply creative job that rewards your imagination and skill. In addition to earning money by actually creating glass products, it's possible for talented crafters to teach their skills to others. This can be a way to make money on the side, or you can try to make it as a full-time instructor.

CHAPTER 8

LEADING IN LEATHER

These days, consumer products can come in all shapes, sizes, and materials. The cheapest options are synthetic, man-made items that can be quickly and easily mass-produced and sold across the world. Despite a growing trend of making things in the least expensive way, there's still a market for traditional leather products. Leather goods made by hand appeal to consumers because of their simple styling, rustic feel, and superior durability. If leather, and its distinctive smell and texture, interests you, why not explore a career as a leatherworker?

WORKED INTO A LEATHER

Leather products are items—from vests to bracelets and more—made from the skin or hide of animals. Cowhide, which is relatively easy to acquire, is used most frequently by both mass-producers and traditional artisans. Leatherworkers also use goatskin, pigskin, calfskin, sheepskin, and steer hide. The type of skin depends on the item being produced and the target price point. Leather has many uses; it has a place in clothing, shoes, belts, hats, furniture, and even sculpture. The potential for leather products is almost limitless.

There are two main types of leather markets: commercial trade and custom leather. Commercial trade includes mass-produced and machine-made items, such as belts, wallets, leather clothes, and furniture. These items are made in the hundreds and thousands and typically sold at affordable prices to

Before a leatherworker can start any project, they must determine which kind of hide they want to use.

general retail consumers. A person in this field will probably work for a large manufacturer.

On the other hand, custom leather products and art leather are primarily handcrafted. Though leather artisans do use machines and technology for some of their work, the majority of the crafting is still done by hand—especially for high-end products. Custom leather is sold at arts festivals, craft shops, galleries, and by commission.

PREPARE TO CRAFT

If you're interested in becoming a leatherworker, you should start early. If your high school offers them, you should take classes that teach you about art, including color theory and general design. If your goal is to become a freelance leather artisan, selling your products to individual clients, you should also consider taking some business or marketing courses. This background knowledge will help you when you try to go pro. Additionally, check out local trade guilds or arts committees. There may be a membership fee to join a professional association, but doing so can connect you with experienced artists and help you learn before you enter the workforce.

There are many different ways of working with leather, and you'll need to understand the basics before you can start crafting. That's why it's so important to take classes and speak with other leatherworkers. Some of the techniques you should know are:

- **Tooling:** Using this technique, leather artisans create a variety of designs with tools that compress the surface of the leather. They rub the tools—which may have pointed, balled, or flat ends—over damp leather to create a pattern, texture, or design.
- **Stamping:** Another way to create a design is by stamping the leather with a copper pipe or large-headed nails. A leather artisan uses a wooden or rubber mallet to press a stamp into damp leather. The leatherworker must be careful that the leather is just the right amount of damp—leather that's either too wet or too dry won't hold the impression of the stamp.
- **Carving:** Moist, natural cowhide, calfskin, or sheepskin are the best choices if an artisan wants to use a carving technique. In the simplest form of carving, the leatherworker uses a swivel knife to cut designs into the leather and a flat, modular tool to press the background. Leather artisans are able to develop their own unique carving styles since there are few rules to follow when decorating leather with this technique.

There are many tools and techniques in a modern leatherworker's arsenal. The best way to learn more about them is to get hands-on experience, whether on your own or as an apprentice to an established artisan.

A CRAFTY LIVING

Much like many other crafting careers, if you want to become a leatherworker, you have several good options. If you choose to work for someone else, whether in a mass-production factory or in a small boutique studio, you'll likely start off making little money and working your way up. As an entry-level leatherworker, you'll be doing basic tasks and practicing your technique. When you improve, you'll be given more responsibility and more creative freedom. This will lead to greater pay and greater opportunities.

If you're interested in being self-employed, you'll likely be able to make more money—but there will also be a lot more risk. You'll have to either buy or rent some studio space, purchase your own tools, and be responsible for client outreach. Though it's easier than ever to sell handmade goods online, that also means there's a lot of digital competition. Your work must stand out from the crowd if you want to be successful as an independent artisan. In addition to internet sales, you'll want to look into joining local arts communities so you can sell your products at craft shows and other events. Leather must be seen and felt to be truly appreciated, so face-to-face time with potential customers will let your work shine bright.

The outlook for leatherworkers is similar to that of many other crafts—growth is projected to be slower than the national average by the Bureau of Labor Statistics. Competition in artistic fields is tough. That said, the market for leather products is strong, and there's always a need for people to craft belts, wallets, purses, shoes, and more. If you can find a position in a company that mass-produces leather goods, you'll likely have a lot of job security.

CHAPTER 9

POKING HOLES

As a tool, the humble needle doesn't look that impressive. However, in the right hands, that tiny piece of pointed metal can work wonders. Needleworkers are skilled artistic professionals who use simple tools to combine thread or yarn with other fabrics for countless purposes. Needlework can be used to add design to a pillow, repair a torn shirt, or create a wall decoration. Though the skills required to become a needleworker can be difficult to learn, you can become a professional artisan without any advanced education. What's more important is your patience, artistic eye, and ability to learn.

STITCH IT UP

Needlework stitchery encompasses a wide variety of styles and techniques. One style is called crewel embroidery or crewelwork. This type of embroidery is made by stitching wool or silk thread on linen, silk, or wool fabric, and it commonly depicts traditional

If you want to become a needleworker, you'll have to work with a wide variety of threads, fabrics, and techniques.

A NEEDLE IN TIME

Because delicate and artistic needlework can be performed with just a few simple items, the art has a long global history. Egyptian tomb paintings show embroidered clothing. The Romans held needlework in high regard, treating it as they would other forms of skilled crafts. Basic needlework stitches haven't changed much over centuries, although the needles used in modern times are very different. Ancient people used bone, wood, or ivory to sew warm, simple clothes from animal skins. Today, needles are made of plastic or steel. Needlework was also used to adorn garments worn by clergymen during the Middle Ages.

In colonial times, samplers like this were often used not just to test someone's ability, but also as teaching tools.

The embroidery was stitched by monks and nuns. The needlework on traditional clothing in Russia and central Europe reflected where a person was from. Homemakers of many cultures have long embroidered household items, including curtains, bedspreads, and towels. Needlework was very popular in America during colonial times. Learning to stitch was part of a girl's education, and she often created a cross-stitched sampler once she had the talent. Samplers were items that featured numbers, letters, poetry, prayers, and artistic designs like flowers—all embroidered with an extreme attention to detail. These colonial samplers were used to teach children to read and write. Many samplers hang in historical societies and museums today, reminders of the beauty and durability of embroidery.

designs, such as leaves and flowers. These designs are typically overlaid on the surface of the fabric, and the needleworker follows the lines to finish the decoration.

Needlepoint is a stitchery technique in which wool yarn completely covers a canvas mesh. The finished piece, which is very strong, has many practical uses. Its durability makes it suitable for use as upholstery, handbags, picture frames, rugs, and slippers. Bargello is one popular example of a needlepoint style. It's recognizable by its bold, elegant geometric patterns. Needlepoint artisans can stitch intricate designs depicting flowers and scenery by working on a tiny mesh called petit point. Skilled needlepoint workers often work with clients to create custom designs that depict family members, pets, or other personal images.

Another way to dress up a fabric is to add beadwork. With this method of needlework, a waxed thread and needle are used to cross-stitch beads onto material or canvas. A bead worker can cover an entire item with beads to produce a striking finished product. These crafts are often more decorative than functional, but there's also a market for beadwork garments.

Knitting is another form of needlework, and it's among the most popular techniques. Using yarn and needles, a knitter can create a huge selection of useful and artistic items, including sweaters, scarves, hats, or blankets to sell at craft fairs or shops.

No matter the technique used to produce them, handmade needlework items can last for years and make wonderful gifts. The yarn and needle are highly versatile artistic instruments, and the more you learn about the world of needlework, the more you'll be able to do with them.

PREPARE TO CRAFT

To learn to do a specific type of needlework, try taking a class at a craft shop or through an adult education program. There are also many instructional books and online resources for anyone who wants to learn the fundamentals of needleworking. Once you're comfortable with a technique or two, you can buy your own equipment (needles, canvas, and a frame if necessary) and experiment with different styles, designs, and stitches. Fortunately, the equipment you need to get started is inexpensive and doesn't take up much space—you can probably do all the practicing you need right in your own room.

Be patient when learning needlework, and start small. Large projects can be overwhelming to a beginner. As you progress, the quality and complexity of your pieces will improve. You should also be willing to experiment with various techniques to create your own personal style. If you decide you want to open your own stitchery, having distinct and unique products will help your business succeed.

A CRAFTY LIVING

Because most mass-produced needlework items are auto-stitched by massive machines in factories across the world, most skilled needle artists work for themselves. Stitchers sell their products at craft fairs, art shows, and online. There are also artist cooperatives where needleworkers (as well as other craft artisans) can market their creations. Some needleworkers are so skilled that they can earn a living by creating customized items to customers' specifications or by producing elaborate works of art. The best way for you to break into this industry is simply to practice and try selling your products on a small scale. After gathering feedback from some of your customers, you can improve your craft and increase sales.

CHAPTER 10

GETTING IT IN FRAME

Have you ever thought about the object that goes around pictures in your home? Picture frames can serve many purposes. At a base level, they protect the photograph, document, or painting contained within. If a frame has been made by a master craftsperson, it can highlight the natural beauty of a painting or add a dramatic feeling to a diploma. Framers are talented crafting professionals who design and create protective and decorative frames for clients who want to add a special touch to important memories and accomplishments.

WHAT'S FRAMING?

There's much more to the craft of picture framing than popping a photo into a store-bought frame. In addition to being patient, artistic, and enthusiastic, a picture framer needs an understanding and appreciation for the many elements that combine to make attractive and protective framing for photographs,

Most frames you can buy in a retail store are mass-produced by machines, and the attention to detail in a master framer's work makes it far superior.

paintings, or important documents. More than anything, framers must enjoy working with their hands and eyes. Helping customers review their framing options for displaying and protecting diplomas, needlework, certificates, and rare documents is a detail-oriented task. Being able to judge proportion, as well as coordinate color, texture, and proportion, are vital to the success of a framer.

Traditional picture framers assemble frames by cutting and assembling molding. They choose the color and texture of mat board and cut mats—or windows—to border and protect whatever's going inside the frame. A framer must be mindful of how the image to be framed will relate to its surrounding.

After the frame itself has been created, framers cut glass and "fit" all the elements cleanly into the protective shell. In addition to preserving the art, a frame and mat should enhance it, bringing out details and colors in art, emphasizing the importance of a document, and making it more attractive to hang on the wall of a home or office.

PREPARE TO CRAFT

If you think framing might be a career you'd like to pursue, you should try to attend industry trade shows. These gatherings of professionals and businesses often offer courses, panel discussions, and general information that could help you take your first steps.

There are specialized vocational schools that offer basic courses for aspiring framers as well. Even if you can't find a place that offers formal instruction, there are educational opportunities available in libraries or online. It's also relatively inexpensive to buy some basic tools and practice framing techniques at home.

To gain some hands-on experience in the craft, a novice picture framer might consider finding a part-time job in a framing shop or at a gallery. Working alongside more experienced framers is an excellent way to observe the art and learn the finer points of framing.

A CRAFTY LIVING

The salary you'll earn as an entry-level picture framer will likely be low. Don't be surprised if your first few jobs offer only minimum wage. However, you also shouldn't be discouraged by a slow start. The framing industry can be tough, but you'll make more money once you've proven your artistic talent.

Skilled picture framers can find work in frame shops, art galleries, and museums. The majority of frame shops are smaller local operations with just a few full-time employees. The owners of these businesses are commonly framers themselves, so you may have to spend a lot of your employment working the front counter. If that's what you're asked to do, you should be polite to customers. Over time—once you've proven you can be a valuable member of the team—you may be able to move to the back room to do some actual framing. Workers in the back room must be organized, detail oriented, good at math, and able to do consistent and accurate work.

If you decide to open your own picture framing business, consider building a customer base by establishing relationships with people in the arts and crafts community. If local artists and craftspeople like your work, your business will expand when they recommend you to their friends, associates, and clients. You may also want to stock your shop with framed prints and decorating accessories for added sales. A framer's work speaks for itself, and if you can impress customers with your style and creativity, success will follow.

CHAPTER 11

GET QUILTING

For many Americans, quilts are objects of both nostalgia and function. In addition to keeping people warm on chilly nights, quilts can remind people of their grandparents or relatives. Many quilts available in the United States have designs that trace their origins back to the early American colonies. Their patchwork appearance and hand-stitched details are just some of the factors that make quilts so unique.

FABRIC MAGIC

A patchwork quilt is typically made in three layers. The top piece is a colorful combination of patchwork squares that have been assembled from many small pieces of cotton. The middle layer is a large piece of cotton or synthetic quilt filling. The bottom layer is a large sheet or plain fabric that's been stitched into a bigger, quilt-sized piece. What most people call quilting is the act of sewing together the three layers with delicate stitches. When the layers are

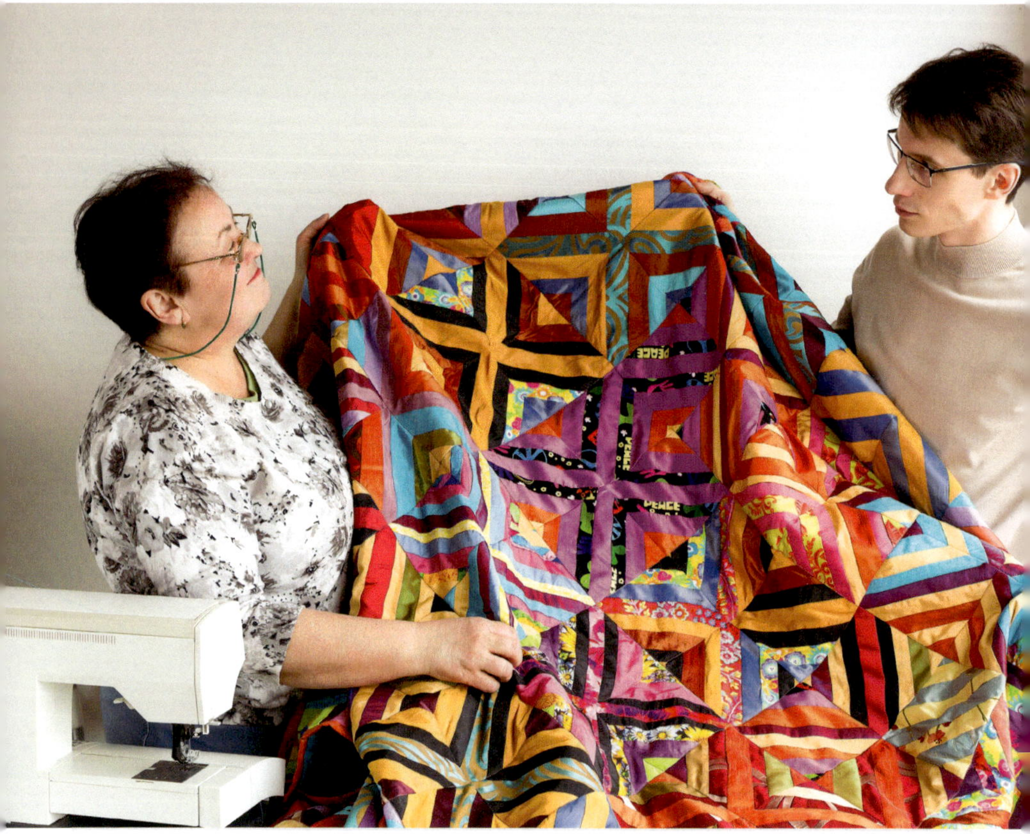

Quilts have a distinctive appearance that can be rooted in the crafting traditions of cultures from around the world.

quilted together, they make a cover that is stronger, warmer, and much more attractive than any of the pieces would be on their own.

Many quilt makers have in-home studios to design and work on their products. While professional quilt makers commonly work alone, others work in cooperatives. There are rarely opportunities to find employment as a quilter in a large company.

You'll need to have a lot of patience if you want to be a quilt maker, even if you choose to sew together the patchwork pieces by machine instead of by hand. In addition to having sewing skills, a quilt maker also needs a keen eye. These craftspeople need to be organized, creative, and neat, with a flair for putting together fabrics and colors in a pleasing way.

PREPARE TO CRAFT

Quilt making is an American tradition, and it's especially popular in the Midwest and rural communities all across the country. If you visit any small town in the United States, there's a good chance you can find a local quilt shop where crafters can buy fabrics and other supplies. These shops are often busy with artistic activity, as quilt makers can gather there to share ideas and take a variety of classes. Some classes are aimed at beginners, while others are tailored to people who have been stitching up storms for years.

In addition to community quilters, there are traveling teachers and artists who travel regionally, nationally, and internationally, spreading the craft everywhere they go. Famous or influential quilters often make appearances at arts festivals, quilting conferences, and other events catering to handicrafters. You should check out some of these gatherings to learn more about the wide world of quilting.

If you're an absolute beginner, the best thing you can do is practice quilting in your spare time. Read up on techniques, watch how-to videos online, and try to get the basics down. You should start

When you're learning the basics, it's best to start with smaller projects so you have room to make mistakes and learn how to correct them.

with smaller projects and slowly work your way up to larger undertakings. Crafting a quilt is hard work, but if you set reasonable project goals, you'll improve your skills and prepare yourself for more serious designs.

A CRAFTY LIVING

There are few opportunities for quilters in large corporations, so you should expect to make money by selling your products directly to consumers. As such, your income will depend on the quality of your quilts—which will determine how much you can sell them for—and how much you can sell at one time. There's no set salary for quilters.

You can also earn money by selling your work through craft shops and entering quilt competitions. Many quilt makers add to their income by repairing other people's quilt tops, teaching, lecturing, writing books, and creating patterns and products. Quilters often get their products placed in local consignment shops, which helps them reach a wider audience while minimizing overhead expenses.

It can be very expensive to open your own physical store, and many small businesses don't survive because of overhead. As online shopping continues to spread, however, you may be able to sell your creations on an arts website or through your own digital storefront. However, keep in mind that you'll have to figure out how to deal with shipping costs if you sell online, either charging your customers or paying the cost yourself. When you're just starting out, consider finding work in a quilting or fabric store where you can help other quilt makers with their creations or give lessons in the craft. You might also run quilting classes at home or teach quilt making in community programs. While most quilt makers see their art as a hobby, there are options available if you want to make the craft your full-time job.

CHAPTER 12

STAINING ON PURPOSE

Regardless of religion, people from all over the world study and appreciate the stained glass art that's a focal point in many churches in Europe and the United States. These colorful masterpieces are made of many pieces of colored glass, separated by thick and distinctive lead borders. The craft of stained glass making is centuries old, but modern techniques and uses are keeping the art form alive. If you've got a lot of patience and a strong attention to detail, you may want to pursue this career.

ADDING COLOR

A stained glass craft involves creating a design that will be pieced together from many small pieces of colorful glass. Stained glass as we know it today is rooted in the decorative religious images embedded in the windows of Europe's cathedrals from centuries ago. When these old crafts were made, the clear glass was colored with a stain.

Centuries-old European artisans laid the groundwork for an art form that now stretches well beyond religious usage.

Eventually, glassmakers were able to incorporate color into the glass by adding minerals and metals during the actual glass production process. Nowadays, people who work with stained glass don't necessarily make the glass themselves. Often, the glass is already made and ready for the stained glass artist to use. Cathedral glass, made by machine, is available in a variety of textures. Opalescent glass has a milky or marbleized appearance. Overlaying a layer of colored glass with frosted, clear, or amber glass creates an effect called flashed glass.

Glass can be etched or sandblasted, which removes its outer layer and creates a design by revealing the layer below. While stained glass is most commonly associated with windows, other products made from stained glass include wall decorations, lamps, lampshades, sun catchers (often placed over windows), and ornaments. When illuminated from behind by light—whether natural or artificial—stained glass adds a soft glow of color to a room.

PREPARE TO CRAFT

With a learning process that's long and time consuming, it takes much practice and patience to become a skilled stained glass artist. Though you can gain some experience by trying out simple techniques on a small scale, the only way to get real hands-on experience is to find work at a stained glass studio. Some businesses offer apprenticeship or internship programs in which you can learn the ropes—but you likely won't be paid.

Another option for beginners is taking introductory classes about stained glass at an art center or community college. It can be expensive to buy all the materials you need to make stained glass at home, so taking a class like this is a good way to practice the basics at an affordable price. Pursuing general art education can also help your stained glass career.

PANE MAKING

The design for a stained glass window begins as a full-size drawing on paper. Sometimes, it's the craftsperson who makes this drawing; other times, the drawing is supplied by a customer or an outside designer.

Colored glass is selected based on the original design and the purpose of the window. The glass is shaped with a glasscutter to fit the shapes depicted in the design. Smooth-jawed pliers are used to cut the glass into shapes that have awkward curves.

To apply a design to glass, an artist uses a mixture of powdered glass and metal oxides that becomes a black or brown paint when combined with water. The artist carefully traces the lines from the original drawing onto the glass. To achieve a shaded effect, the stained

Creating stained glass artwork is a matter of patience and craftsmanship. Using a variety of tools, artisans can make complex, colorful designs.

glass maker uses a thinner wash, which is then left on the glass to dry. When it's ready to be fired, the glass is loaded into the upper part of a kiln. The extreme heat in the kiln fuses the paint to the glass. However, the high temperature also strains the material, so it's necessary to leave the glass in the kiln to cool slowly.

In traditional stained glass panels, lead is used to edge each piece of glass because it provides a strong, flexible bond. The lead is cut and bent to match the contours of each piece.

Learning about colors, design principles, and material choices will give you a good background once you break into professional stained glass making.

A CRAFTY LIVING

The salary for stained glass artisans varies according to their experience and the quality of their work. The stronger your work, the more likely you'll be to find a job at an existing studio. Getting a position like this has its advantages. The best part about working for a stained glass studio is job security and a steady income. You know your paychecks will arrive on time in a consistent amount. On top of that, you'll have room to advance if you continue improving your stained glass crafting skills. However, working for someone else has its disadvantages too. That's why some crafters prefer to work as self-employed artisans.

Freedom is the underlying theme of self-employed stained glass makers. They're free to set their own schedule, workload, and prices. That also means they can set their own pay—so if you're talented, you should be able to make more money than if you worked at a studio. The downside of self-employment, however, is inconsistency. You can have down months, and if the industry turns for the worse, you won't have much of a safety net. You'll also be responsible for buying your own materials, renting a physical space or paying for an online domain, and any taxes and fees that go along with running your own business.

CHAPTER 13

TEXTILE STYLE

Historians believe that some form of weaving has been part of every developing civilization, though its exact origin in human history is unknown. Few clues from ancient societies have survived. Primitive humans likely wove together sticks and reeds to make clothing, blankets, hammocks, rugs, pouches, and other useful everyday items. By definition, weaving is the craft of interlacing two sets of threads. Today, rugs, table linens, wall hangings, and clothing are just some of the textiles that weavers craft. If you have an eye for color and texture, you're patient, and you're good with your hands, you may be interested in exploring this ancient art form.

WOVEN IN HISTORY

In modern weaving styles, the craftsperson attaches one set of threads—called the warp—lengthwise on a loom. The warp threads must be parallel and an equal distance from each other. The weaver guides the horizontal threads—called the weft—over and under the warp threads, passing them crosswise from one side of the warp to the other, and back again.

Before beginning work, many weavers like to sketch their designs on small sheets and then enlarge the drawing to the intended size. To do this, the weaver draws a grid over the first drawing and then draws a grid on a larger sheet of paper with the same dimensions as the design. They then copy the squares from the smaller grid onto the larger grid in the corresponding area. This enlargement is called

One of the most important tools in a modern weaver's kit is the loom. This large piece of equipment takes a lot of skill to learn.

a cartoon. The cartoon is pinned behind the warp and traced with a marker. The weaver is then able to transfer the cartoon directly onto the loom, helping guide their weaving.

Almost any kind of material can be woven. Wire, strips of fabric, leather, yarn, and even paper can be interlaced to form beautiful designs—as long as the craftsperson has the talent to do so. From the materials and weaves, an artisan can create geometric, striped, and countless other patterns.

The plain weave, sometimes called a tabby weave, is extremely simple. To do it, the craftsperson weaves the weft over and under the warp threads, making sure they alternate the pattern with each row. This type of weave can be done tightly or loosely, depending on the material, the type of work the weaver is trying to produce, and the look they want to achieve.

The basket weave style is accomplished following a technique similar to a plain weave. With the basket weave, however, two warp threads are interlaced with two weft threads. When this is done with two different colors, the result is a classic checkerboard pattern.

PREPARE TO CRAFT

To become a weaver, you must be very patient. Learning to weave, especially if you're starting with complex techniques, can take a tremendous amount of time. Most weavers have rooms set up in their homes that are dedicated to the craft. Looms can be large, so it's a good idea to find a space that can accommodate one.

Before you buy any equipment, however, you should first find a way to learn more about the craft. Many arts centers and community colleges offer basic weaving classes and may even provide you with the materials you need to get started. You should also look up weaver's guilds and see if there are any nearby. Even if not, you can reach out to professional organizations through email or social media, and members will be happy to give a beginner some guidance. In addition to learning the basics of weaving, you should take this educational period to find out if you actually like the craft. It takes a lot of patience to become a professional weaver, so it's better to find out early if a career in textiles is not for you.

A CRAFTY LIVING

Weavers, like most craftspeople who are self-employed, don't have a standard or consistent salary. As a beginner, you likely won't earn much money. However, as your skills improve, you'll be able to sell more products at higher prices. There are even some weavers who command hundreds or thousands of dollars for their work—though they're the best of the best.

Most weavers sell their work at craft fairs and galleries or from their studios. Some crafters open an online store or sell their handiwork through other digital storefronts. Weavers can also teach, work at shops that sell weaving supplies, or write books and articles to supplement their incomes. These options are good if you're having a particularly slow month, you're a beginner, or you just want to mix up your daily routine.

A select few weavers earn large commissions to produce enormous crafts that will hang in public spaces, such as hotels, office buildings, airports, or theaters. You shouldn't go into weaving because you expect such widespread recognition, but trying to earn a large commission is an admirable goal for any crafter.

CHAPTER 14

WOOD YOU PLEASE?

When most people look at a tree, all they see is an ordinary piece of nature. If you have the soul of a crafter, however, you may look at a tree and see an endless realm of possibilities. For centuries, humans have designed, shaped, polished, and experimented with wood to create countless useful items—some of which are still in use today. Though cheaper materials like plastic are widespread in industries that traditionally used wood, such as furniture, there's still an undeniable demand for the craftsmanship and nostalgic feel of a handmade wooden table or chair. If you think you have what it takes to transform trees into treasure, a career as a woodworker may be for you.

THE RIGHT TOOLS

The fruits of a woodworker's labor have many uses. Sometimes, their creations are meant for decoration. Other times, they have a more practical use.

Woodcrafters may carve animals, statues, figures, and walking sticks, or they may construct cabinets, bookcases, tables, chairs, or doors. Wooden objects add natural beauty and proven functionality to a space.

It's impossible to shape wood with your bare hands, and the tools of a woodworker are many and varied. Woodcarvers typically work by hand, using tools such as chisels and knives for a lot of the shaping and finishing work. However, power tools are also an important part of most woodworking projects

Skilled woodworkers require a lot of equipment. Their tools are used for both shaping and finishing products.

at some point or another. The machines commonly found in a woodshop include sanders, lathes, and various types of power saws. These advanced technologies make some parts of the craft easier, but the finishing touches—including most detailed work—is still done with hand tools.

PREPARE TO CRAFT

Believe it or not, it's possible to start learning about woodworking from a young age. Many high schools offer woodshop classes for students who may be interested in turning that craft into a career. In addition, check the offerings at local adult education programs and colleges. If you're fortunate enough to know a woodworker personally, you can ask them for an apprenticeship. Though you likely won't be paid for your labor, working under an experienced craftsperson can teach you invaluable skills that can be used later when you're trying to find a paying job.

The skills required to become a successful woodworker are basic, but they take time, energy, and hands-on practice to master. If you want to explore this career, your first stop should be a local library. Because this art form is so old, there are countless instructional books packed with information that can benefit you whether you're a complete beginner or a seasoned pro. There are also many online resources that can teach you the basics of woodworking, the skills you'll need, and the equipment you'll use.

Whether you're working in an existing woodshop or starting out on your own, make sure to handle all your equipment and materials safely. Everyone knows power tools can be dangerous if used incorrectly, but the same is also true for hand tools. It's one thing to accidentally hit your finger with a hammer, and another thing to cut open your hand with a chisel. When in doubt, exercise caution and take it slow. Learning to woodwork is a long process.

A CRAFTY LIVING

Whether you're working for someone else or as a self-employed crafter, your compensation as a woodworker will be closely connected with your personal skill and professional experience. If your products are well made, you'll be able to sell them for more money. This will, of course, increase the amount of money that goes into your paycheck. Your salary will also be determined by your woodworking specialization. The more popular your products, the more you can sell.

Cabinetmakers hold many of the jobs in the woodworking industry. They specialize in building wood cabinets for homes and businesses. Other professionals in this specialization may work in factories or workshops. Sometimes, cabinetmakers build cabinets on-site; other times, they build cabinets in their workspace and install them later. Cabinetmakers must be precise with their measurements.

Cabinetmaking is one popular woodworking specialization. These craftspeople create and install custom cabinets that can increase the value of a home.

In addition to getting the technical details right, cabinetmakers can express their more artistic sides when creating a design. Consulting with their client, they can choose the wood or finish that will be applied to the cabinets.

Woodturners shape, polish, and cut wood into decorative creations. They primarily use lathes to

gradually shape the wood into a wide variety of objects, from bowls and boxes to sculptures and table legs.

Guitar makers can work for companies that manufacture high-end guitars, or they can craft guitars in their own workshops. Acoustic and electric guitars are commonly made from rosewood, spruce, mahogany, or cedar.

Toy makers use wood to create toys that last for years. Handcrafted toys often outlast their plastic counterparts and make unique gifts. Wooden toys are among the most popular items at craft fairs. A skilled woodworker in another specialization might branch into toy making to expand their offerings.

Whichever field of woodworking you want to specialize in, there should be positions available for you. It's true that cheaper materials are often used, and some companies use machines to fashion wooden products, but there's nothing that can replace the look and feel of a handcrafted wooden masterpiece.

GLOSSARY

apprentice Someone who learns a trade by working with a skilled person of that trade.

consignment shop A store that pays the supplier of an item after it sells.

consistent Always happening the same way.

contemporary Modern; present-day.

crucible A container in which metals or other materials are heated to very high temperatures or melted.

distinctive Having a unique or special characteristic.

distinguished Making something seem important and worth respect.

durable Able to last for a long time.

embellish To decorate or adorn.

guild An association or group formed for the aid and promotion of common interests.

heirloom A possession handed down from generation to generation.

kiln A furnace or oven used for baking or firing pottery or ceramics.

loom A hand-operated or power-driven device for weaving fabrics.

marketing Promoting a product or service.

porous Having small holes through which light, air, or fluids can pass.

significant Very important.

standard Following customs or rules.

supplement To add; to make up for a lack of something else.

symmetrical Having sides or halves that are the same.

textile A kind of cloth that's woven or knit.

traditional Following what's been done for a long time.

translucent Not fully clear or transparent but clear enough to allow light to pass through.

vocational Of, relating to, or undergoing training in a skill or trade to be pursued as a career.

wholesale Relating to the business of selling things in large amounts to other businesses.

FOR MORE INFORMATION

American Craft Council (ACC)
1224 Marshall Street NE, Suite 200
Minneapolis, MN 55413
(612) 206-3100
Website: https://craftcouncil.org
Facebook, Instagram, and Twitter: @CraftCouncil
This nonprofit organization helps spread arts and crafts all across the United States, hosting craft shows and conventions to spread awareness and increase education.

The Association for Creative Industries (AFCI)
330 North Wabash Avenue, Suite 2000
Chicago, IL 60611
(312) 321-6811
Website: https://creativeindustries.org
Facebook: AFCI.Global
Instagram and Twitter: @AFCI_Global
The AFCI is a professional organization that's involved with education and outreach for people working in—or hoping to work in—artistic or creative businesses.

The Canadian Bookbinders and Book Artists Guild (CBBAG)
180 Shaw Street, Unit 102
Toronto, ON M6J 2W5
Canada
(416) 581-1071
Website: https://www.cbbag.ca

The CBBAG has provided support for the development of book arts since 1983. Its website has information about book-related crafts and educational opportunities for artists.

The Corning Museum of Glass

1 Museum Way
Corning, NY 14830
(800) 732-6845
Website: https://www.cmog.org
Facebook: @corningmuseumofglass
Instagram and Twitter: @corningmuseum

Opened in 1951, the Corning Museum of Glass is one of the most respected glassmaking institutions in the country. It offers glassblowing demonstrations and hands-on experiences with the craft.

FUSION: The Ontario Clay and Glass Association

1444 Queen Street East
Toronto, ON M4L 1E1
Canada
(416) 438-8946
Website: https://www.clayandglass.on.ca
Facebook, Instagram, and Twitter: @FUSIONclayglass

Working with various Canadian artistic organizations, FUSION offers education and professional support for clay and glass crafters.

Handweavers Guild of America (HGA)

1255 Buford Highway, Suite 209
Suwanee, GA 30024
(678) 730-0010

Website: https://weavespindye.org
Facebook: @HandweaversGuildofAmerica
Instagram: @instahga
Twitter: @weavespindye
This trade organization's goals include educating people about weaving, promoting existing artists, and connecting professionals in the textile arts. HGA also produces an international arts festival every other year for fiber crafters.

Society of American Florists (SAF)
1001 North Fairfax Street, Suite 201
Alexandria, VA 22314
(703) 836-8700
Website: https://safnow.org
Facebook and Instagram:
@SocietyofAmericanFlorists
Twitter: @safdelivers
This professional organization represents those who make a living with flowers. The SAF website offers information for growing your business and learning more about the industry.

FOR FURTHER READING

Boy Scouts of America. *Pottery*. Irving, TX: Boy Scouts of America, 2016.

Felix, Rebecca. *Cool Leatherworking Projects: Fun & Creative Workshop Activities*. Minneapolis, MN: Checkerboard Library, 2017.

Kallen, Stuart A. *Careers If You Like the Creative Arts*. San Diego, CA: ReferencePoint Press, 2020.

Levete, Sarah. *Maker Projects for Kids Who Love Woodworking*. St. Catharines, ON: Crabtree Publishing, 2017.

Meadow, Katie. *Crafting with Flowers: Pressed Flower Jewelry, Herbariums, Decorations, and Gifts for Every Season*. New York, NY: Skyhorse Publishing, 2020.

Meinking, Mary. *Start Your Crafting Business*. Oxford, UK: Raintree, 2018.

Santore, Marcia. *Craft Artists: A Practical Career Guide*. Lanham, MD: Rowman & Littlefield, 2020.

Shaw, Carole Lyles. *Madly Modern Quilts: Patterns and Techniques to Inspire Your Quilting Creativity*. Bradenton, FL: Modern Quilter Media, 2016.

INDEX

ABOUT THE AUTHOR

Siyavush Saidian lives with his wife and two corgis in New York. A lover of books and writing, he knew college was the right path for him, but he realizes that's not the case for everyone. He's excited to help young people find jobs they love, just like he did.

CREDITS

Cover (main image) DashaR/Shutterstock.com; cover (icons) Natasha Pankina/Shutterstock.com; p. 7 Portland Press Herald/ Getty Images; p. 10 Fotogloria/Getty Images; p. 15 Costantino Costa/Getty Images; p. 16 photoL/Getty Images; p. 21 Falcona/ Shutterstock.com; p. 24 Gekko Gallery/Shutterstock.com; p. 28 Shi Yali/Shutterstock.com; p. 31 Jacob Lund/Shutterstock.com; p. 36 DangBen/Shutterstock.com; p. 39 Boogich/Getty Images; p. 42 Rawpixel.com/Shutterstock.com; p. 45 UfaBizPhoto/ Shutterstock.com; p. 49 Benoit Daoust/Shutterstock.com; p. 53 itakefotos4u/Shutterstock.com; p. 55 Pixel-Shot/ Shutterstock.com; p. 58 AnnaStills/Shutterstock.com; p. 61 Steve Allen/Shutterstock.com; p. 62 AntiMartina/Shutterstock.com; p. 67 Roman Samborskyi/Shutterstock.com; p. 72 melnikof/ Shutterstock.com; p. 74 PHILIPIMAGE/Shutterstock.com; p. 78 Pack-Shot/Shutterstock.com; p. 80 eFesenko/Shutterstock .com; p. 84 David Talukdar/Shutterstock.com; p. 89 Syda Productions/Shutterstock.com; p. 92 ungvar/Shutterstock.com.

Designer: Brian Garvey; Editor: Siyavush Saidian